"Grief: Is This Normal?" *By Diana M. Cimador Roscigno is a powerful and incredibly well written book. It presents the questions that all parents face when the tragedy of their children's death faces them. The book offers practical strategies to help parents understand and identify the emotional, physical and spiritual changes that bereaved parents face in this journey. One of the most important aspects that the book makes readers recognize is that as painful as this is, you are not alone. The author does a great job of explaining that the feelings, emotions and unanswered questions bereaved parents face are normal,... and the author does a phenomenal job making this point crystal clear. The book is loaded with many tools and wonderful explanations of concepts that only a parent put in such a difficult position could ever explain. The author does this with grace, class and tremendous integrity.*

Most importantly, "Grief: Is This Normal?" *truly helps parents verbalize the questions and the roller coaster of emotions that they have about the unknown.*

"Grief: Is This Normal?" *is an exceptional book for anyone looking for insight from a parent's perspective on the death of his or her child. I was moved by the content and highly impressed with the reader-friendly, warm, and intelligent writing style.*

I very highly recommend it as a must read book for bereaved parents and practitioners who work with these individuals."

George Giuliani, PhD., Author

"Grief: Is This Normal?" *Diana Roscigno has written a primer on grief...the grief for a child...more intense than any other. In her first book,* "1 Am Still His Mother", *the reader experiences first hand the raw, gut wrenching pain and disbelief of such a loss. Her story shares with the reader her own shock and disbelief, and the questions she suddenly must deal with...how does she survive such incomprehensible loss? Where does she turn for answers? What does she do with such unrelenting pain?*

In "Grief: Is This Normal?" *Diana shares what she has learned from her experience. For the newly bereaved this is both a validation of the myriad of confusing thoughts and questions that play endlessly in our minds and a workbook to help sort through that confusion. Reading it, one recognizes the identical questions and experiences every bereaved parent must cope with. It assures us that we are not alone, that such responses and questions are common after surviving the loss of a child... that indeed, there is a new normal in the world of the bereaved parent.*

Finding hope again, after the death of a child, is a lifelong journey. In sharing all that she has learned about love, forgiveness and survival since the death of her beloved son Mark Anthony, Diana shines a beam of light into a world that might otherwise seem to have become forever dark.

~ Marie Levine, Author,
"First You Die: Learn To Live After The Death of Your Child"

I read Diana's book as a newly bereaved parent. It was one of many I read, however it carried with it a style of writing quite candid. This book addresses frightening issues newly bereaved parents face.

The confirmation of many of these feelings, combined with the words to identify them and tools to address them makes this a book to read.

Maria Gloria Verdile's mom, Holly, Bereaved Parent.

"Normal? The only thing that is normal about grief, aside from the need to grieve, is that it isn't normal. Even in a shared sorrow it still is very personal, mine, and we wander aimlessly, often feeling very alone, isolated, misunderstood.

Diana Roscigno knows the walk and the talk from her loss of a son and brings it together in this outstanding guide for the sorrowing.

It is all about that which seldom is normal, but user-friendly, comforting and hope filled. Certainly it is what I need at the moment."

Rev. Richard B. Gilbert, PhD., CT, Author

GRIEF

Is This Normal?

for bereaved parents

Diana M. Cimador Roscigno

ISBN 0-7414-4588-3

Published by:

INFI∞ITY
PUBLISHING.COM

1094 New DeHaven Street, Suite 100
West Conshohocken, PA 19428-2713
Info@buybooksontheweb.com
www.buybooksontheweb.com
Toll-free (877) BUY BOOK
Local Phone (610) 941-9999
Fax (610) 941-9959

Printed in the United States of America

Printed on Recycled Paper

Published April 2008

DEDICATION

MARK ANTHONY GOVERNALE

June 20, 1985 – January 1, 2003

"Until we meet again my son
May you soar the Heavens
On angels' wings"

And

In honor of all children
who have died too soon

ACKNOWLEDGMENTS

To my husband, soul mate and life partner, Paul.

For all we've been through good times or bad and everything in between. You've gone the extra mile more times than I can count.

You have been so loving, patient, kind, understanding and supportive of my endeavors as I continue to reach out to other bereaved families.

Dad, your guidance and love have given me the strength to follow my heart and dreams. A`PŪNTO.

Lisa Marie, my beautiful daughter, you are my sunshine and so dear to me.

Thank you so much for all of your help and support.

Live life, laugh, dare to make your dreams come true.

I love you more each day Tish.

Markie, you are unforgettable, an inspiration and the wind beneath my wings.

You are forever part of me and everywhere I am.

You continue to make a difference in the world.

A special thanks to:

Alan Pedersen, Ashley's dad, composer of, "A Little Farther Down The Road".

Blakely's mom, Barbara Russell

Kaylee Rose Conlon's mama and dada, Amy and Ed

Maria Gloria Verdile's mom, Holly

Peggy and Denis O'Connor's mom, Elaine Stillwell

Peter's mom, Marie Levine

Rev. Richard Gilbert

Dr. George Giuliani

CONTENTS

INTRODUCTION

The loss of a child is unfathomable, incomprehensible and undeniably life altering.

Parents are not supposed to bury their child.

This book offers insight and a better understanding of a newly bereaved parents grief journey.

It will identify many of the emotional, physical, behavioral and spiritual changes that can and often do occur on a newly bereaved parent's grief journey.

Within these pages you will find helpful material offering comfort, guidance and hope for healing.

For those who have not suffered the loss of a child, this book will educate you about the complexities of parental grief and hopefully make it easier for you to understand and be supportive of bereaved parents.

By sharing what I have personally experienced and learned on my grief journey along with the knowledge that I have gained by attending gatherings, conferences, workshops, programs and from listening to other bereaved parents and their families, this book will benefit whoever reads it.

SOUND FAMILIAR?

Individually, one's grief journey is as unique as one's fingerprint, yet we share many of the same feelings.

These changes, reactions and responses are natural, necessary and normal.

As strange as they all seem, they are a true expression of where you are on your grief journey.

The void in your heart, mind, soul, body and spirit feel unbearable and consuming.
It cripples the core of one's being and existence.

There may be a lump in your throat, a hollow empty feeling in the pit of your gut or a void that can't be filled.

You can't comprehend your life without your child in it.

You long for and miss your child beyond words.

This isn't right.
It isn't fair.

You want someone to wake you up from this nightmare.

It doesn't seem real.
Your mind simply rejects the idea that your child is dead.

You don't want to do this anymore.

You want things to go back to the way they were.

You want your child back.
You just want your child back.

You try to escape grief's clutches, but can't.
It is always right there, just below the surface.

Waves of grief leave you breathless and in what feels like never ending pain and suffering.

There is no motivation or desire to do anything.

Everyday is a challenge.

You take one step forward and fall back two.
Hang in there. It's not always going to be like that.
It does get better.
You are wherever it is that you need to be on your journey.

A roller coaster of emotions leave's you dazed, in a fog like state, unable to focus and easily distracted.

If you think you are going crazy, that's normal.

Tears that arrive uninvited and that are uncontrollable are known as "Grief bursts" or attacks, melt down or bullet days.

Questions will go unanswered and you will keep asking them until you don't have to anymore and that's okay.

Why did this have to happen?

Where is my child now?

Is my child safe, in pain or suffering?

Is my child at peace?

Is there really life after death?

Will I ever see my child again?

Can my child see me?

Will I receive a sign?

Why did God take my child?

Why didn't God take me?

Am I being punished?

What do I do now?

What am I supposed to do?

Who am I now that my child has died?

Am I still my child's mother or father?

What is life's meaning and purpose?

Will I survive?

How?

Will my family survive?

Will I ever smile again or laugh?

How can I be happy when my child is dead?

How long am I going to feel like this?

Will it ever get better?

Is it ever going to end?

How do I do this?

Is what I am feeling normal?

NOTES

IS THIS NORMAL?

You are entitled to ask yourself if what you are feeling and experiencing is normal or abnormal.

There are many factors and variables that influence and impact a newly bereaved parent's grief journey.

They can include:

How your child died (sudden, prolonged illness, miscarriage, stillborn, murder or suicide)

How you were told and by whom

The child's age, birth order and sex (for the bereaved parent the age of the child that has died has no relevance)

The wake, funeral services or rituals

Your Personality

Your age (influences your ability to understand death and dying)

Sex (gender grief is real, men and women just grieve differently)

Your relationship (with your child)

Past deaths

Unresolved loss

Myths

Life's stressors (home, family, career, spiritual and cultural beliefs)

Finances (funeral expenses, medical bills)

Your health

The change of seasons

The weather

The time of the day

Expectations of the grief and mourning process

How you work your grief

Support network (check what resources are available and surround yourself with people who will allow you to grieve your way)

These are just some of the many factors and variables that can create differences in your grief process.

Your grief is as individual as you are and the circumstances surrounding your child's death.

Grief is our natural way of responding to our loss.

Grief is a journey that is experienced, endured, processed and expressed through our emotions, feelings, thoughts, reactions and responses.

It is normal to feel a wide range of emotions when you are grieving the death of your child.

Give yourself plenty of time to experience all that accompanies your loss.

There are no timelines on this journey.

Working your grief requires both listening and being heard.

You cannot outrun grief.

You can't even hide from it.

It will find you.

Expect the unexpected.

It has a way of creeping up on you out of the blue, usually when you least expect it.

There is no quick fix.

There is no magic wand.

There is no way around it.

There is no way above or below it.

The only way is through it.

This is much easier said than done.

Resisting, denying or suppressing your grief will only send it underground temporarily and delay the grief process.

No one can take away your pain or suffering.

No one can grieve for you.

It is your child who has died.

There will be times when you'll want to get off this roller coaster that is spiraling out of control and paralyzing you with fear, or times when you'll feel like you have been knocked down by a wave.

Everyday is a challenge to feel alive, when your world has crumbled and nothing is as it once was.

Life is a daily struggle.

You want things to go back to the way they were, but the harsh reality is that they can't.

Your child is dead forever.

May you find some comfort in knowing that the intensity of your pain and suffering will not last forever, it becomes tolerable.

Validation and confirmation lets bereaved parents know that they are not alone.

NOTES

GRIEF EXPECTATIONS

Physically, grief is brutal.

Emotionally, grief is battering.

Sometimes the simplest things of everyday life seem frivolous and unimportant when your child has died.

It's an effort to get out of the bed or function on any level.

You have no appetite at all or eat everything in sight searching for comfort in food.

If you have no appetite eating small frequent healthy amounts of food may be helpful.

Your body needs to be nourished and hydrated (drink plenty of water).

You become a lamenting couch potato or keep busy to have a welcome distraction.

You feel like you have aged overnight.

You sleep too much or not enough.

You return to work.

Frustrations mount when your expectations of family, friends and co-workers are not met.

Perhaps it is unrealistic to expect them to know what they can do to help, when you yourself don't know what that is.

As you discover and understand your "New Normal", you will be better able to make your needs known.

Family and friends are not mind readers.

There probably have been times when family or friends have called and you haven't answered the phone because you just weren't up to it.

Not being able to take a call can be misinterpreted and may send the wrong message.

They don't realize how difficult it is for you to hold a conversation, especially when you are having a bad day.

Usually within the first few months of your journey you'll begin to notice that calls and cards from family or friends start to dwindle.

Your address book will change.

Receiving calls or cards, especially around the holidays, your child's birthday or anniversary date, let you know that your child has not been forgotten.

Grief makes people uncomfortable.

Bereaved parents often say they feel like an alien and are avoided like a plague, as if the death of their child is contagious.

People look or act differently around and toward you.

Family and friends want you to go back to the person you were before your child died.

Knowingly and unknowingly, family, friends, and even strangers, can and do say something hurtful or insensitive to your loss.

Sometimes, it may just be something to say when they don't know what to say.

Other times, it may be an attempt to diminish your loss or take it away from you.

Conversations will usually shift or change when your child's name is mentioned.

This may be because they think that by mentioning your child's name it is causing you more pain or it may be too painful for them.

Speak up.

Give them permission to say your child's name.

Let them know that hearing your child's name is music to your ears.

Hearing your child's name let's you know that your child is thought of and remembered.

You never want your child erased or forgotten.

It is important to surround yourself with the support of people who will allow you to grieve and mourn your loss.

You wonder how long you are going to feel this way or how long it will take until you feel better.

You can't imagine going on like this and you struggle to free yourself from grief's quicksand.

You search for comfort.

You may solicit the services of a medium, psychic or rely on cultural, spiritual and religious beliefs for the answers you are looking for.

There is a need to know where your child is, that they are safe, not in any pain or suffering.

You may even allow yourself to be fooled into thinking that your child is at school, on a playdate, traveling or studying abroad.

It's hard to comprehend or grasp how life goes on all around you as if nothing has happened.

You feel like you are going crazy.

You're not.

You're grieving the death of your child.

You want or need confirmation or validation, that what you are going through and experiencing is "Normal".

Will you ever get over this?

No, but you can overcome it.

You have a choice.

How do you move forward?

Cautiously.

These are uncharted waters.

You can nurture your grief or just tread water.

Be patient with yourself and others.

Do only as much as you are able.

This is your journey.

There are no timelines.

No two people grieve exactly alike.

No one can take your grief away from you or do it for you.

It is your child that has died.

You'll learn that "Grief bursts" (uncontrollable involuntary tears) can be triggered by anything, a smell, sound, sight, taste, touch, place or a memory.

You avoid triggers that arouse your grief.

Grief does not allow you to think clearly.

You have difficulty staying focused or completing a task.

You become less productive.

It is a good idea to put off any major decisions and not make hasty ones, for example moving or changing jobs.

Scattered, your thought process is all over the place.

You may start a sentence and lose it midstream.

Your mind wanders.

You may go into a room to get something or open the refrigerator and forget what it was that you were looking for.

That's normal.

You may feel like you are in a fog, like a fish out of water or like a bumper car bouncing off one wall only to hit another.

How will you survive?

How are you supposed to live without your child?

Check out the resources that are available in your community, Bereaved Parents of the USA, The Compassionate Friends, hospices or outreach programs.

A support group atmosphere should be a safe haven; one of acceptance, understanding, caring, friendship, comfort and hope for healing.

Support groups allow you to be in the company of others who are like you and seasoned grievers who have not only survived, but have reinvested in living life again.

It takes a lot of courage to walk through those doors and understandably so.

Never in your wildest dreams did you ever think that you would be in a room filled with bereaved parents.

This is not a group you elected to be a part of.

You expect the people in the room to be more like you.

What is wrong with them?

How can any of them be happy when their child is dead?

You may even think that you are in the wrong place, want to turn right around and walk back out that door or find yourself sitting through a meeting ready to crawl out of your skin.

You may even want to leave, but hesitate because you don't want to call attention to yourself.

Don't be discouraged if you feel worse after you attend your initial meeting.

It is normal to feel that way.

You may want to try a few different groups until you find one that you are most comfortable with.

Sooner or later you will be faced with what to do with your child's belongings?

You may become over protective of them or not want to part with them.

They are all you have left.

Your home or your child's room may become a shrine.

It's not unusual to have pictures of your child in every room.

You may leave your child's room left untouched complete with dirty laundry in the hamper.

There may be times when you'll find yourself hugging your child's pillow, blanket, toy, or sniff your child's clothing hoping to smell their scent, so that you can feel closer to them.

You may wrap yourself up in your child's favorite blanket.

These are just a few of what are otherwise known as linking objects.

Don't let anyone push you into doing anything with your child's belongings that you are not comfortable with.

Take your time.

There is no hurry to do anything with them.

They can be put in a storage bin or sealed bag for safe keeping until you are ready to go through them.

Wait until you are ready.

You may want to give some of your child's belongings to family or friends as keepsakes or donate them to someone less fortunate.

Huggable soft cuddly stuffed bears can be made with fabric from your child's clothing or favorite blanket.

Again, this can be done later on.

The choices are yours to make.

You will find ways to keep your child's memory alive.

You don't want your child erased.

You don't want your child forgotten.

Make a quilt or have one made for you.

Craft stores have an assortment of iron on decals or items that can be sewn on.

Photographs can be transferred to fabrics or any number of other photoproducts, such as ornaments, mouse pads, throws, mugs, canvas or jewelry, the list goes on and on.

Make a shadow box or scrapbook.

Find the way that works best for you.

Right now, you have all to do to just make it through another day.

Some days are endless.

Other days are fleeting and gone before you know it.

Try as you might, there is no escaping grief.

You can duck and dodge all you want; there is no escaping grief, it is always right there.

Your grief journey will not be without pain and suffering.

To move forward you will need to go toward the pain and through it, not away from it.

You may cry for hours, sigh, sob or not shed a tear and that's okay.

It is important to understand that your tears are a release, cleansing, healing, and exhausting.

They are healthy and are not a sign of weakness.

You may feel alone, lost, confused, bombarded, bewildered and overwhelmed by the wide range of feelings, thoughts and the emotions that you are experiencing.

You don't know if you, your marriage, your family or relationship with a significant other can or will survive the death of your child.
It hurts to see each other in pain.

You may expect your spouse to know what you need from them and when you need it.
Anything short of that leaves you feeling unloved and not supported.

Actions or lack of action can easily be misinterpreted.

Sometimes your partner cannot be there for you the way you need for them to be.

How do you make this better?

Keep the line of communication open.
Reach out and learn from each other.

Men tend to channel their grief into the workplace, hobbies and sports.

They appear to be less willing to be open and talk about their grief.

They see themselves as providers, protectors and Mr. Fixit.

There is a sense of urgency heard in their voices when they say to me, "Please tell me what to do, I don't know how to make my wife feel better".

They can't fix this.

It's easy to get caught up and forget that you cannot take each other's grief away or do it for each other.

Women on the other hand, tend to be the nurturers or caretakers and they channel their grief differently than men.

It is difficult to take care of your own grief work when you are so busy trying to help and be there for other family members.

Women tend to discuss and express their grief more openly.

You may become overprotective of loved ones.

Respect each other's space and right to process their grief in their own time and way.

Be patient, kind and supportive of each other.

As important as it is to listen, it is equally as important to be heard.

Answers to the following questions may be helpful.

What would you like to know from your spouse or significant other about his or her grieving?

What can you do to help?

What would you like them to know about your grieving?

What is a difficult part of your grief journey that you are dealing with now?

NOTES

THE FIRST OF EVERYTHING

There is no denying that the first of everything is hard.

The first time you say your child has died.

The first time you go into your child's room.

The first time you go through your child's belongings.

The first time you part with something that belonged to your child.

The first time you see that empty seat at the table.

The first time you realize that your child is not coming home.

The first time you visit the cemetery.

The first time you talk to your child in their absence.

The first "Grief burst" or trigger.

The first time you look at a photo album, watch a video or listen to a tape that has your child's voice on it.

The first time you receive mail addressed to your child.

The first time you hear your child's name called out in a crowd.

The first time someone asks you how many children you have.

The first time you feel like you have received a sign from your child.

The first time you sense or feel your child's presence.

The first time you dream about your child.

The first time you read a book on how to survive the death of a child.

The first time you go to a support group meeting.

The first time you notice the change of the seasons.

The first snowfall, spring bloom, summer barbeque or fall blanket of autumn leaves.

The first birthday, holiday, anniversary, Mother's Day, Father's Day, milestone year or special event such as a graduation, wedding or birth.

The first time you sign a card and struggle with how to include your child's name.

The first time you start a new tradition.

The first time you go on vacation.

The first time you watch a sunrise or sunset.

The first time you smile or laugh.

The first time you do something in memory of your child.

All of these are reminders that your loved one, your child is not present.

The first of everything helps you discover strengths you didn't even know you had and just how resilient you are.

A count down may commence in the days leading up to the first anniversary date.

There is anticipation that if you can just make it to the first anniversary you will feel better.

Do you avoid being home and get away?

Do you just want to get it over with or have a celebration of life?

Will the second year be different than the first of everything?

Undoubtedly, the answer is yes.

How could it not?

Many people express a sense of relief when they have survived the first of everything.

WHAT IS THIS "New Normal?"

No one willingly embarks on this journey and the following is a list of words that you may or may not identify with.

Find the words that best describe you.

They are a reflection of how you are feeling or have felt.

You may want to circle the words that apply to you in the book, jot them down on a separate piece of paper, or write in the space provided.

Doing so will identify the words that are most meaningful to you at that particular time.

Revisit the list as often as you feel there is a need to and freely change, delete or add words.

Remember that your grief needs and feelings are ever changing as you grow and heal on your grief journey.

Abandoned

Abused

Acceptance

Acknowledgement

Adjustment

Afraid

Aged

Agitated

Aggravated

Alive

Alone

Ambivalent

Amends

Anger

Anguish

Annoyed

Anxious

Appalled

Arrogant

Avoidance

Betrayed

Bitter

Blameful

Bothered

Broken

Chaos

Cheated

Cherished

Choice

Closure

Comfort

Conflict

Confrontational

Courageous

Cowardly

Crazy

Cross

Crushed

Cry

Cursed

Dead

Deceived

Denial

Depleted

Depressed

Desire

Despair

Devastated

Diminished

Disappointed

Disbelief

Disconnected

Discontent

Disloyal

Dismayed

Disoriented

Distracted

Distress

Drained

Dread

Empathetic

Empty

Envy

Exasperated

Exhausted

Expectations

Exploited

Explosive

Failure

Fatigued

Fearful

Finality

Forgetful

Forgiveness

Free

Fulfilled

Furious

Guilt

Happy

Harassed

Hateful

Healing

Heartache

Helplessness

Hesitant

Hollow

Hopeful

Hopeless

Horror

Hostile

Humor

Hurt

Idealization

Ignored

Impaired

Impatient

Incensed

Indifferent

Indignant

Indulgent

Insecure

Insulted

Intolerant

Irritated

Isolated

Jealous

Joy

Kindness

Laughter

Lifeless

Listen

Logical

Lonely

Longing

Loss

Lost

Love

Mad

Mean

Meditative

Memorialize

Miserable

Moody

Negative

Nervous

Numb

Obstinate

Offended

Optimistic

Out of Control

Outraged

Overwhelmed

Overcome

Pained

Panic

Patience

Peaceful

Perplexed

Perturbed

Pining

Powerless

Pressure

Provoked

Puzzled

Rage

Rant

Rave

Recovery

Reflect

Regret

Reinvestment

Rejected

Relief

Repressed

Resentment

Restless

Ridiculed

Sad

Scared

Scarred

Scattered

Self Doubt

Sensitive

Serene

Shame

Shock

Smothered

Sobbing

Spiritual

Stress

Stoic

Sulky

Surprised

Surreal

Survivorship

Talkative

Tearful

Tense

Ticked off

Threatened

Tolerant

Tormented

Torn

Transformation

Undecided

Understanding

Unreal

Uptight

Victimized

Vindictive

Vulnerable

Volatile

Withdrawn

Worried

Yearning

POSSIBLE EMOTIONAL CHANGES

Shock and Numbness undeniably shield and protect you from the incomprehensible, unbearable, heart-wrenching intense pain that is felt when your child dies. It lasts for as long as it is needed.

It allows you to go through the motions, and handle arrangements, the wake, Shiva or funeral services.

You may or may not recall the wake or funeral services.

You may have felt dazed, stunned or even in a dreamlike state.

Your mind hears, but it doesn't listen.

You know that you were there, but felt like you weren't.

As the shock and numbness wear off you come face to face with a multitude of emotions.

It's okay to be bewildered by what you never would have thought possible.

You hurt more as you accept the harsh reality that your child has died.

You may feel like you are losing it.

I mean really losing it, like you are going crazy and have lost control of your life.

You are not going crazy.

You're grieving.

Parenting books didn't prepare you on how to survive the death of your child.

Denial allows your mind to retreat from reality. It allows you to avoid your pain.

The mind simply rejects the idea that your child has died.

It doesn't want to open the vault where complicated emotions are stored.

If you cannot accept that your child has died then you cannot mourn and grieve the death of your child.

Deny your emotions, you deny the essence of life.

Fatigue and exhaustion are constant companions.

The simplest things during the course of everyday living can and do deplete energy.

It is an effort to get out of bed, dress, brush your teeth or hair, answer the phone, engage in conversation, eat, drink, run a household, work, and remember to breathe.

Day to day tasks seem frivolous and non-essential.

There is no motivation or desire to do anything.

Shopping, cooking and housework are not high on the priority list.

Take out is always an option.

Dishes can be piled high in the sink and laundry in the hamper.

Errands to the grocery store, bank, post office or cleaners can be done by well meaning family or friends.

So, when they ask is there anything I can do, let them do the shopping, prepare a meal for your family or pick up take out, do a load of laundry, car pool or baby-sit, the list can go on and on.

It is easy to curl up under the covers or on the couch.

You may feel tired, be unable to sleep, have a restless night or want to sleep all of the time, day and night.

You may want to discuss the possibility of a sleeping aid with your doctor.

Scattered, your thoughts jump all over the place.

You may not be able to concentrate for periods of time, focus, read, balance a checkbook, are easily distracted, experience an inability to remember things like appointments, the time, day, month, year or to pay your bills.

Our first Christmas following our son's death, I bought my husband a card that read Merry Christmas To My Wife!

It's common to open the refrigerator or go into a room and then forget what you were looking for.

Leaving the house with different colored socks or shoes on, or putting your shirt on inside out is, "Normal".

There may be increased difficulty, making decisions at home or in the workplace.

Avoid making hasty decisions.

Your productivity will likely not be what it was at home or in the workplace after your child dies.

It is a good idea to keep a pen, pad and a date-book on you at all times.

Have a calendar centrally located in your house to post all appointments (the kitchen is usually a good place).

Keep a pad, pen, journal or notebook on your nightstand.

It may help on a sleepless night to write your thoughts down to induce a restful state of mind.

Have a duplicate set of house, car and office keys.

An automobile club membership comes in handy when you've locked your keys in the car.

Use of a timer is good practice when baking in the oven, cooking on the stove or having a BBQ outside.

It's a lot cheaper than replacing burnt pots, pans and wasting food.

Don't be hard on yourself for not completing things you set out to do.

Be realistic and set attainable goals.

If you get one out of the three things on your list done than you have accomplished something.

Anger is a very real part of the grief process. It reminds us that we are alive. It can be directed at anyone, your self, spouse, significant other, your deceased child, immediate family members, extended family, friends, employers, healthcare providers, emergency response teams, law enforcement, clergy, congregation or even strangers.

You may direct your anger at one or more persons at a time.

It is easier to be angry then to be sad.

Anger is hurtful not just to you, but to others as well.

Anger is heard in the tone of your voice, by what you say and how you say it.

It is also seen and felt through silence and your body language.

If anger is suppressed it can lead to feelings such as isolation, betrayal, desertion and nightmares.

It will compromise your health and prevent resolution of your grief.

Anger consumes time and energy.

It is important to identify what triggers your anger and who are the targets of your anger.

You can be angry with your child.

How could you be angry with your child?

Some triggers may come from self-blame, frustration, mood, anxiety, sleep disturbances, revenge, hate, rage, fear, underlying hurt, resentment, helplessness, failure to receive desired support from family or friends and so on.

Anger is a roadblock and needs to be dealt with in a positive, constructive way, neutralized and channeled, exercise, walk, journal, cry, meditate, do yoga, gardening, paint, sports (bowling, kick boxing, football) photography or even household chores.

A plan of action for anger is to let it out.

Unless you work it, it will leave you stuck and unable to move forward on your journey.

When you begin to feel angry, breathe deeply, take a time out, count, adjust your expectations and decrease the anger by implementing change.

Name it and claim it.

Often anger rises when family and friends say clichés like, "It's God's will, they are in a better place, time heals, think of what you have, you are holding up so well, you have to be strong for others or you can have other children".

Though well intended, these are not constructive and can be painful.

Bereaved parents are often too hurt to respond at that moment.

If and when you are able to respond starting with I, is helpful. For example, I got angry when I heard you say…

The bottom line is to find what works for you.

How does your anger affect the people around you?

(Space has been provided for your response)

What are some of the ways you channel your anger?

(Space has been provided for your response)

Guilt, real or imagined, is a normal part of a grief journey.

It is hiding in many grief closets and is another one of grief's roadblocks.

It can eat you up and spit you out.

It is toxic, postpones, limits, delays and diverts the grief process.

Nothing evokes feelings of guilt like the death of a child.

There are many types of guilt.

You may feel guilty for feeling relieved when your child dies after a long illness, or completed suicide.

You may feel guilty over bad thoughts or fights that you had.

There are always regrets for things said, unsaid, done, and undone.

There is survivor guilt.

Why wasn't it me?

This isn't fair.

You are not supposed to out live your child.

It is natural to think that you could have done something to prevent the death of your child.

If you could have, you would have.

You are human. Remember that.

Guilt has a way of haunting, misleading and manipulating us.

It passes judgment and punishes you for your perception of wrongdoing.

If you perceive yourself as guilty, then you are, until you decide otherwise.

The "If only, I should have, maybe if, I never got to or what if," condemn and torment.

Identify what it is that you feel guilty about.

Ask yourself if the guilt you are experiencing, is based on misdeeds or wrongful intent?

Most often guilt is not rational.

Guilt also needs to be dealt with in a positive, constructive way, or it will keep you from moving forward on your grief journey.

What thoughts, feelings, or actions trigger your guilt?

(Space has been provided for your response)

Finishing the following sentences may be a tool that can help you work through your guilt:

If only…

What if…

I should have…

Maybe if I had…

I never got to…

Some suggestions for handling guilt are:

Be truthful as to why you feel guilty.

Identify what triggers your guilt and why.

Consider the harsh reality that even if you did do something differently, it may not have changed the outcome.

Reduce self-punishment.

You did the best you could.

There are many types of guilt.

Educate yourself.

Write or talk about it.

Let it go.

Attend support group meetings.

Seek professional help.

Focus on the positives in your relationship with your child; the joys, and laughter shared and places you visited.

When guilt is experienced and released you can become open to forgiveness.

Forgiveness can come after processing emotions, lessening your hurt and anger.

Divorce and estrangement issues can complicate the grief process.

Forgive yourself for any wrongdoing you feel you did.

In doing so, forgiveness will free you of guilt's bondage.

It is a cleansing process.

People often misunderstand and think that by forgiving someone their action or wrongdoing is condoned.

This is not the case!

Forgiveness does not condone, approve of, or forget a harmful act.

It does not change the past, but it does change the future.

It means that you open your heart and mind to forgive and to be forgiven.

How different would your life be with forgiveness in it?

(Space has been provided for your response)

Sadness is usually accompanied by an empty hollow feeling in the pit of your gut, a gnawing aching void, a sense of incompleteness.

It is natural to feel sad when you embrace your pain.

Someone you love has died and you are hurting.

You are entitled to feel sad.

It's okay.

Sadness may intensify and can be triggered particularly around the child's, siblings', parents' or grandparents' birthdays, anniversaries, milestone years, or special events (graduations, weddings, births) etc.

It may be worse on the weekends when you are not distracted by running a household, going to work or school, at night when you go to bed or when you wake up in the morning to yet another day without your child.

Your life is full of reminders of your child, their favorite clothes, book, color, food, toy or television show, the list goes on and on.

Cry as freely and for as long as you need to.

Crying releases built up tension.

Tears are healing, cleansing, a healthy expression of grief and not a sign of weakness as thought.

Your tears have a voice.

Listen to them.

Tears can console your heart.

"Grief bursts" (uncontrollable tears) make others uncomfortable and can be embarrassing if they occur in a public place, for you or others.

Expect the unexpected.

They can happen anywhere, at the grocery check out, in a restaurant, on a bank teller line, in a dentist chair, at the mall or while watching a television commercial.

The car and the shower seem to be popular places to let it all out.

A roll of paper towels in the car may work better than a box of tissues.

Depressed, who wouldn't be? Your world as you knew it no longer exists. Hopes and dreams are shattered.

The reality is that you cannot go back in time to the security and comfort zone of what was.

You have had enough, want things to go back to the way they were and to be with your child.

You just want to be with your child.

That's normal.

You may think that you don't deserve to be happy or have a right to experience the joy of laughter when your child is dead.

Family and friends respond differently than expected. By appearances they may seem or appear to be unaffected by the death of your child.

Life goes on as usual.

What is wrong with them?

Don't they realize that your child is dead?

How can they be happy when your child is dead?

Socially, sometimes it is easier to retreat.

Avoid the use of alcohol and recreational drugs.
They stop or delay your grief process.

Prescribed medications can help with depression, anxiety, or sleep disturbances when taken under the supervision of a physician.

If you have suicidal thoughts seek professional help immediately.

Anxiety may lead to avoidance of situations.

You may find that you startle easily.

Your heart may race.

You may feel flushed, experience tightness in your chest, a lump in your throat, shortness of breath or an uneasy feeling.

You may also find yourself feeling hypersensitive, meaning that you are very sensitive to everything going on around you.

It is important and helpful to identify what increases your anxiety and also what helps to relieve it.

What increases your anxiety?

(Space has been provided for your response)

What helps to relieve your anxiety?

(Space has been provided for your response)

Fear of losing another loved one in your life is heightened.

Terrible tragedies happen to other people and now they have come to you.

There is fear of the unknown and the realization that nothing is for certain.

There is a fear that your child will be forgotten.

You can't bear the thought of losing anything pertaining to, or connected to your child.

They are linking objects, treasured and forever keepsakes.

There is a fear that you will make the wrong decisions or choices.

There is fear that you won't survive the first year.

The losses you may experience are many.

There is a loss of control, security and direction.

You don't know which end is up or what to expect next.

There is a loss of family structure.

Be aware of the impact that your child's death has on your entire family, you, your spouse, surviving siblings, grandparents and extended family.

Adjustments are made as new relationships within your family are developed.

Do your part to encourage communication, grieving, openness and expression of feelings.

Communication is key.

Holidays, birthdays, anniversaries, and special events can be particularly stressful times.

Consider the entire family when planning these days.

Siblings are also known as, the forgotten survivors, within a family.

Be sure that they feel loved and included.

Their inclusion in the planning lets them know that they are still an important part of the family.

If the deceased child is not your biological child, your grief for the child is just as necessary, normal and real.

Traditional and non-traditional families, adoptive, step or foster parents, non-custodial parents and grandparents all have a right to grieve and have their grief acknowledged.

It is difficult to care for yourself when you are helping other family members on their grief journey.

Be sure to allow yourself some alone time and space to meet your own emotional needs.

It is important to take some time out of your day to take care of you.

Even if it is just fifteen minutes a day, make that commitment to yourself.

You may find it easier to fulfill that commitment by setting a particular time of the day aside just for you.

There is a loss of identity of self, and purpose, not just the loss of your child.

There is a part of you that you gave to your child that is gone.

Who are you now?

Who you are, includes what you did for, and with your child.

You'll search for life's new meaning and purpose as you discover your "New Normal."

Relationships with family and friends change.

When you are in shock, numb with pain or denial, you have no idea what you need or want.

Especially when well-intended family, friends or co-workers say, "Let me know if there is anything I can do to help".

You expect family and friends to know what you need from them and how they can help.

Usually within months of your child's death you begin to notice that contact by family or friends begins to dwindle.

It may be around this time that the shock and numbness start to fade, you are faced with a multitude of emotions and need a network of support.

Family and friends don't know what you need or what they can do to help.

It is up to you to tell them how they can help.

That is, of course, when you have been able to figure out what that is.

Take the initiative and help them to learn how to support you.

There is a loss of future, unfulfilled plans, dreams and memories you didn't get to create.

Talking about your child gives others permission to do the same.

You have a right to grieve what was, is, and will never be.

To do otherwise would only inhibit your growth and put the brakes on your grief work, processing and journey.

Fearing that your future will be as painful as your present is normal.

Acceptance does not mean that you like what has happened.

It does mean living in the present.

While it acknowledges your loss, it is not submission.

It gives you permission to move forward and take treasured moments with you.

Growth comes with acceptance.

Hope is something you seek out and hold onto tightly, despite the pain, suffering, and sorrow experienced with the death of your child.

A sense of purpose and meaning will and does return. The pain and its intensity do lessen.

You can live a full life again, as the person you are in the here and now.

Hold onto that glimmer of hope.

It's a life preserver.

Hope is your beacon of light in the darkness.

POSSIBLE PHYSICAL CHANGES

Fatigue and exhaustion

Chronic aches and pains

Sighing

Sleep disturbances, too much, too little, difficulty falling asleep, staying asleep, nightmares, dreams or flashbacks

Your immune system becomes compromised and you may find yourself getting sick more frequently

A balanced diet, rest and moderate exercise is especially important at this time

Under-active (like a couch potato)

Overactive (can't sit still, constantly on the go)

Changes in appetite lead to weight fluctuations, gains (Comfort food) or losses

Digestive changes

Nausea or vomiting

Crying, sobbing or weeping

Dehydration (dry eyes, nose, mouth, skin), drink plenty of fluid and moisturize your skin

Muscle aches, twitches or tremors

Knees buckle

Headaches or migraines may be relieved by meditation, music, medication, compresses, acupuncture or massage

Decreased sexual desire

Heart-aches

Rapid heart rate, pulse, palpitations

Tightness in chest

Lump in throat

Dizzy

Unsteady gait

Startle easily

Increased sensitivity to surroundings

POSSIBLE BEHAVIORAL CHANGES

Go through the motions of daily living

Change of routines

Sudden mood changes

Alcohol and drug abuse

Diminished self-care, stay in pajamas for days, poor hygiene, forget to brush your teeth or shower, wear the same clothes for days

Cry

Avoid situations that arouse your grief

Avoid triggers

Keep busy

Go to a supermarket or stores that you didn't go to with your child

Binge shopping may result in excessive debt and doesn't fill the void

Forget to pay your bills

Address books change

Family, friends and co-workers don't act as we expect
or know what to do for us

You may experience a decreased desire for
conversation

Withdraw and not partake in festive occasions

Make your needs known, when you know what they are

Give family, friends and co-workers permission to say
your child's name

You don't want your child forgotten

Make a shrine

Carry an object that belonged to your child

Wear clothing of your child's

Assume mannerisms and interests of your child

Set a place at the table

Customize a license plate

Talk to your child

Tell your story over and over again

Write a letter to your child or in a journal so you can see your progress

Look at pictures and videos or listen to your child's voice on a tape (make copies)

Make albums, memory jar, memory book, memorial web site, create scholarship fund, foundation, organize blood drives, walk-a-thons, bike-a-thons, golf outings, volunteer your time to a homeless shelter, food pantry, hospital, hospice etc. or make a donation in your child's name to the charity of your choice

Attend candle-lightings, balloon launches, tree of memory dedications, butterfly releases, walks to remember or plant a serenity garden

Visit the cemetery, or not at all, some find it comforting, others not

Look for a sign (pennies from heaven, birds, rainbows, butterflies, feathers, dreams)

Explore psychics or mediums

Bury your head in books or not at all

Question how you are going to survive and what to expect

Reach out for help (attend a support group where you'll meet someone who has been where you are, understands the depth of your despair and who has survived)

POSSIBLE SPIRITUAL CHANGES

The death of a child challenges one's faith and beliefs

Pray

Being angry with God or your higher power, is normal

Distrust faith

Cast doubt

Ask questions:

Why?

What did I do to deserve this?

Is this God's will?

If God loves me then why did he take my child?

Where is my child?

Is my child okay?

Does my child see me?

Will I ever see my child again?

What will happen when I die?

Is there eternal life?

Feel abandoned by God, Church, Clergy or Congregation

Unable to attend church

Attend everyday

Decreased spirituality

Increased spirituality

Betrayed by life's cruel twist of fate

Search for a meaning and purpose in life

Sense loved one's presence (hear, smell, feel, see)

Look for signs that your loved one is around (pennies from heaven, a feather, butterfly, dragonfly, bird) etc...

Feed your spirit

THE PATH TO HEALING

The path to healing is through your pain.

The healing process is one that requires active participation.

The key to this transition is you.

Healing comes when you allow yourself to openly express your grief.

What you feel you can heal.

It doesn't happen overnight or by itself.

It takes work.

It takes hard work everyday and making choices that will encourage and promote healing.

Working your grief is essential for healing.

It means that you acknowledge your child's life and death.

It means accepting what you cannot change.

However, that doesn't mean that you have to like it.

You won't ever like it.

You can't go back to who you were before your child died, however, you can live a full life as who you are now.

You want to make your family "Normal" again.

Doing that means acquiring the skills and tools needed not just to survive, but also to reinvest in living life again.

It means educating yourself and others, reading books, articles, attending workshops, seminars, conferences, gatherings or support groups.

Remember to take what you want and to leave the rest behind.

It means telling and retelling your story.

There is no timeline when you are grieving the death of a child.

It takes however long it needs to take and that's okay.

We are reminded of timelines that society sets with clichés like, "It's been a year now or why aren't you over it"?

To that I answer my child is still dead.

They don't realize that this is a lifelong process.

Ready or not bereaved parents can and do return to work.

Life must go on.

Sometimes a part time job can be a welcome distraction for a stay at home parent.

Time can and does heal, but that depends on what you do with it.

Bereaved parents do experience and endure a unique blend of emotional, physical, behavioral, spiritual changes, reactions and responses.

It's okay to be confused by what you feel and experience.

This may include:

Did I in some way contribute to my child's death?

Am I going to forget my child's face, smile, voice, smell or touch?

I don't want to be here.

I miss my child.

Things will never be the same.

How do I survive?

How am I going to get through this?
I want someone or something to tell me how I am supposed to do this.

Am I going crazy?

I feel so helpless and hopeless.

I can barely function.

I have no drive or ambition to do anything.

I don't care about anything anymore.

I don't know what to do with my child's belongings?

Did I fail as a parent?

NOTES

HELPFUL SUGGESTIONS

Take up a new hobby, garden, cook, knit, crochet, needlepoint, embroider, quilt, journal, scrapbook, photography, draw, paint, sketch, meditate, exercise, walk the dog, do art therapy, crafts, puzzles, bowl, golf, yoga, horseback riding, sing, volunteer, go to movies, read poetry, write a book, learn to play a musical instrument, dance, kick-box, boat, fish, swim, play a sport, skydive, hang glide, cycle, bird watch, hike, travel, white-water raft, stroll on a beach or find ways to get more in tune with nature.

Journaling can be done in many different ways.

The type of journal and pen you choose does make a difference.

If you are not comfortable writing in a journal there are other alternatives.

For instance you can make an arts and craft type of journal, draw or sketch in your journal.

Another option is to use a voice recorder.

Make copies of photographs, videotapes, audiotapes, or important documents pertaining to your child.

They can't be replaced.

Take measures to preserve them in a bin, metal container or safe deposit box.

Documents can be laminated.

Use acid free paper to protect your photographs and in scrapbooks.

These are precious keepsakes.

Each time you go shopping try to extend the amount of time you are able to be in the store.

You may start with ten minutes and a list with two or three things on it. If you get one of the three pat yourself on the back.

Gradually increase the amount of time that you are able to be in the store and the amount of items on your list.

Going during off peak hours to shop helps avoid crowds.

You might also want to try going to stores that you had not gone to with your child.

If your local grocery store delivers take advantage of the opportunity.

Another option is to buy holiday or special occasion gifts by shopping by catalog or online.

You may be more comfortable visiting the cemetery when it is less crowded.

Release stress with a good cry, massage therapy, aromatherapy, candles, oils, long baths, showers, hot tub, meditation, yoga, acupuncture or even pet therapy (which provides unconditional love, companionship and exercise).

Laugh, laughter reduces stress and is a sign of healthy coping.

Listen to music or make your own.

Dance.

Seek support from family, friends, co-workers, clergy, therapists, community resources that are available, support groups, hospices or outreach programs.

Support groups promote healing, encourage acknowledgement of your child's death, the expression of your grief in an atmosphere of acceptance and understanding. It is where you will find other bereaved parents with similar experiences.

Tell and retell your story.

Find someone who is willing to listen 24/7 and willing to be a sounding board for as long and as often as you need.

There will be times when having someone present is enough for you to lean on or to receive a reassuring bear hug.

It is important to have a good network of support.

Preparing for upcoming holidays and special events isn't easy.

They are a painful reminder that your child is not present and that your circumstances have changed.

Usually, the anticipation of the holiday or special event is worse than the day itself.

Traditions may make you uncomfortable, become triggers and painful reminders.

You may want to consider not doing some of them this year, resuming them next year or starting some new traditions.

Include your child on cards by using a photo stamp or return address label with your child's picture on it.

Holiday photo greeting cards can include your child by holding a framed picture of them or placing one so that it is visible in the family portrait.

If you have a tree or garden in memory of your child, you might want to consider decorating it and taking a family picture there or at a favorite place you shared with your child.

How do you include your child's name on a card?

It may be too difficult for you to write your child's name.

Use an angel or butterfly stamp on greeting cards.

You can also use butterfly or angel stickers.

Find the way that works best for you.

You need family and friends to understand that you may have to limit family and social commitments.

If you are feeling pressured to partake in festivities and if you are not up to it or able, then don't.

Decline the invitation.

Be flexible.

Fluctuations will occur.

Have a plan A and B for backup.

Take your own car or go with someone who won't mind leaving early if you need to, or RSVP that there is a possibility that you may leave early and would like to do so without drawing attention.

Giving an angel, butterfly, photo-ornament or snow globe, to family and friends each year is a great way to have your child remembered at holiday time.

You can write your child's name and the year on them.

Every year when those ornaments or globes are taken out your child will be remembered.

Memories will be happy and sad.

Include your child's name in conversation.

Don't be surprised if people change the subject and there may be some awkward moments of silence.

Give people permission to talk about your child.

Invite family or friends to write a favorite memory of your child, poem or quote that remind them of your child.

You can put them into a scrapbook, memory jar, box, holiday stocking, or on a memorial web site.

Surround yourself with people who will listen, understand and support you.

Do what is right for you during the holidays and special events.

Memorializing your child can be done in so many different ways.

Maybe you'll establish a scholarship fund or foundation; plant a tree of memory, serenity, meditation or butterfly garden, dedicate a garden bench or plaque, volunteer at a local hospital, soup kitchen or shelter, have a star named in memory of your child or adopt a spot locally.

Become a mentor; volunteer your services to the Boys and Girls Club, Little League, Scouting, or a charity that may have been of interest to you or your child.

If your child suffered from a prolonged illness, you may request that donations be made in the memory of your child to a children's hospital or hospice.

Have a blood drive, clothing, food or toy drive.

Donate a gift to someone less fortunate.

Spearhead productive change's such as; contribute defibrillators at athletic events, modify drunk driving laws or install rear view cameras on SUV's.

Make a donation to Bereaved Parents of the U.S.A. or The Compassionate Friends.

This enables these organizations to continue to reach out to newly bereaved families.

Donate a book to a local chapter's lending library in memory of your child.

Learn the skills and tools necessary that will teach you how to cope, ease your pain, survive, find hope for healing, reinvest in life and move you forward on your grief journey.

Share what you know.

Educate others.

Become a facilitator to other newly bereaved parents.

Write a book.

Anything is possible.

NOTES

FINAL THOUGHTS

The grief of a bereaved parent is the most intense grief known.

The love and bond that you shared with your child transcends their death.

Bereaved parents will always be the parent of the child who has died.

Grieving is a transition, a transformation.

Do you ever "get over" the death of your child?

No.

This is not something you just "get over".

You will never get over the death of your child, but you will get through it.

Will your world ever be the same without your child in it?

No.

Your child's death will be with you all the rest of your days.

However, so will your child's life.

You will be challenged to discover who you are now that your child has died and what is referred to as your "New Normal".

If you don't give yourself permission to mourn and grieve, you will stay frozen in pain, immobilized and your life will have stopped where your loss left you.

By allowing yourself to feel and experience grief's most intense heart wrenching pain can you move toward a life in which pain, is not the center of your world.

Each of us makes choices that will determine how we process our loss and our grief journey.

You have a responsibility to try to heal some of the hurt inside of you.

Nurture yourself, get plenty of rest, eat nutritious healthy meals, lighten your schedule and do what you need to do to take care of you.

Working your grief can mean that the bad days will gradually become less.

The good days will come more frequently and last longer.

Sharing your grief with others won't make it disappear, but it will make it bearable.

Time can heal, but what really matters is what you do with time.

It is up to you to become a willing and active participant of your grief journey.

What you feel you can heal.

You know that you are making progress when you can remember your child's life rather than your child's death.

This usually happens when the wound is no longer raw or open and has formed a scar.

You know that you are making progress when you can survive even though you didn't think you could.

You know that you are making progress when life makes some sense again and you can enjoy it.

Death ends a life, but certainly not the relationship or the love shared.

It forces life to begin anew.

Embrace it.

You are not alone.

I hope you have found this book to be informative, supportive, understanding, comforting and that it has given you some hope for healing.

It has been a pleasure to serve and share with you.

May you not only survive your loss, but also heal and grow because of it.

"Although the world is also full of suffering, it is also full of overcoming it"

Helen Keller

May our children's light always shine.

NOTES

A Little Farther Down the Road

I know those tears you're crying
I've been in your shoes
You feel like there's no use in trying
Like there's nothing left to lose
You take one step forward and move two steps back
You may not see it now but it won't always be like that

A little farther down the road
You'll see the sun again
A little farther down the road
You'll look back at where you've been
And you'll see how far you've come
And you'll find the strength to go
A little farther down the road

This journey is not easy
It's a winding road filled with twist and turns
But you can make it believe me
In time you'll learn
That a greater love comes from your deepest pain
And there's power in that love to help you rise again

By Alan Pedersen © 2005 EverAshleymusic

In Memory of Mark Anthony

(Written to him, for him and about him)

I AM

Crying behind this mask of mourning
Tears hidden beneath its disguise
Invisible to the world around me
There are no answers to the question why
So I have stopped asking

I let you go
I let you fly
and
You paid the price
With your life

No longer estranged our we

For in your death
Forgiveness has set us free
We share a bond you and I
As only a mother and son could have
Forever that will be so

My tears are for the remnants of
Tomorrows shattered dreams
I mourn for the loss of
What might or could have been
Life has such a different meaning now

ou be forgotten
Nev
ives you touched
By

The warmth of your love is captured

Forever in our hearts

Cherished and embraced in

Tomorrows summer shade and

Winter's necklaces

Until we meet again my son

May you soar the

Heavens

On angels' wings

I love you so very much

By Mark Anthony's mom, Diana M. Roscigno
Remembering his Twenty-first birthday

GRADUATION DAY

Not for you my son
This being your
Twenty-second year
Instead what should be your
College Graduation Day
Remains a dream and wish
That our hearts made

There will be no Pomp
And Circumstance
No Cap, Gown or School Ring to order
No party to plan
No pictures to take
Commemorating the Celebration
Of yet another one of
Life's milestones
Achieved and Embraced

Graduation Day forever will be
That of Middle School
Your confident stride
And grin that beamed with pride
As you received your Diploma
You gave me a rose

Bear hug
Kiss
And said,
"I Love You Mom"

Graduation Day
Forever will be
A memory of one of
Life's Precious Moments
A priceless gift
A treasured keepsake

How grateful I am for that
Graduation Day

By Mark Anthony's mom, Diana M. Roscigno
June 2007

YOU'RE 22 TODAY

The thought of ever losing you forever
Never crossed my mind
Not from the moment
I gave birth to you
Twenty-two years ago today
Until
The day you died

The harsh reality stares back at me
From your tombstone
Mark A. Governale

I no longer deny what once felt so surreal
When everyday was a challenge to feel alive

It reminds me that tomorrows
Are
Taken for granted and shouldn't be
To live in the moment
In
The presence of today
And
I strive to do just that

You are with me
In every breath I take
Tears I cry
In my dreams
And
In all that I do

Time has a different meaning now
So does what I do with it

Happy Birthday Son
Happy Birthday Markie

Thank you
For the love and the memories
Of a lifetime shared

You are and always will be the love of my life, my light,
An inspiration and unforgettable

"Until we meet again my son
May you soar the
Heavens
On angels' wings"

By Mark Anthony's mom, Diana M. Roscigno
Remembering his Twenty-second birthday
June 20, 1985 – January 1, 2003

THE PITCHERS MOUND

Provides a better view at 5:30 a.m.
As I stand in wait for this morning's eclipse

My canvas shoes are wet
From the morning dew
Your camera in my hand
I'm ready to document
The canvas of this morning's sky

Unexpectedly, bittersweet memories
Set the stage for a burst of
Uncontrollable tears
That suffocating lump in my throat
That all consuming hollow void
And piercing crippling pain
My heart aching to see you,
Touch, smell or hear your voice
Just once more

Moments like this these remind me
Not just of how loved and missed you are
But also of how cheated I feel
For you, me, all of us
Life had a much different plan in mind
You see

Not one that either you or I
Could ever have imagined
When you once stood on this
The pitchers mound

My tears are swept away by
The memories of yesteryears when
I can recall
Your teammates surrounding you
After throwing the winning pitch
So confident and proud you stood on
The pitchers mound

New memories are in the making
Just in a different way now
Son
You are always with me
Even right here, right now
As I stand on
The pitchers mound

By Mark Anthony's mom, Diana M. Roscigno
The morning of August 28, 2007

"THE RENAISSANCE MAN"

What are human gifts?

I think I can safely say and think at this very moment that most of us do not dwell on the topic too often. God provides messengers in this area in unique ways sometimes softly and sometimes with extreme intensity – even most tragically. We all have these beautiful gifts in varying degrees, but do we recognize that Godly reality? The Renaissance was an explosion of thoughts, deeds and accomplishments. The Sistine Chapel is the epitome of mans wondrous ability to think, do and accomplish. One would argue that nothing is impossible – even landing a man on the moon.

It has been my experience in life that those born with a preponderance of Godly gifts are most humble about the situation – they just do, no matter what the challenge.

When I think of Mark, I think of these human gifts. He was extremely bright, extremely dedicated to task be it academic, physical sport, scouting, music, love of nature, plus his complete tenacity of deed to such – again, in a most unassuming manner.

Yes, I always refer to Mark as a Renaissance man. He truly is and will always be that to me.

By Mark Anthony's grandfather, Fausto R. Cimador

GRIEF RESOURCES

Alive Alone
1112 Champaign Drive
Van Wert, Ohio 45891
Email: alivalon@bright.net
Support for bereaved parents whose only child or all children are deceased

American Association of Suicidology
2459 South Ash Street
Denver, CO 80222
(303) 692-0985
www.suicidology.org
Supplies literature and referrals to survivors of suicide

Bereaved Parents of the USA
National Headquarters
P.O. Box 95
Park Forest, IL 60466
(708) 748-7866
www.bereavedparentsusa.org
Bereaved Parents of the USA (BP/USA) is a nationwide organization, offering self-help support groups for bereaved parents and their families who are struggling to survive after the death of a child. Any bereaved parent, sibling or grandparent is eligible to become a member of BP/USA.

Centering Corporation & Grief Digest Magazine
PO Box 4600
Omaha, NE 68104
(402) 553-1200 or 1-866-218-0101
www.centering.org or www.griefdigest.com

Comfort Zone Camp, Inc.
80 Park Street
Montclair, NJ 07042
Toll Free: 1-866-488-5679, Ext. 120
Tel. #: (973) 364-1717
www.comfortzonecamp.org
Comfort Zone Camp is the nation's largest camp program for children 7 years old to 12th grade, who have experienced the death of a parent, sibling or primary caretaker. Approximately 60-70 children attend each camp weekend – for free!

The Compassionate Friends
P.O. Box 3696
Oak Brook, IL 60522-3696
(877) 969-0010
www.compassionatefriends.org
Information and resources for families who have experienced the death of a child

Concerns of Police Survivors (COPS)
P.O. Box 3199, S. Highway 5
Camdenton, MO 65020
(573) 346-4911

www.nationalcops.org

Support for law enforcement officers and their families who have been affected by death and bereavement

Mothers Against Drunk Driving (MADD)

511 E. John Carpenter Freeway, Suite 700

Irving, Texas 75062-8187

1-800-GET-MADD

www.madd.org

Education, resources and advocacy for bereaved families

National SHARE office

300 First Capitol Drive

St. Charles, MO 63301

(800) 821-6819

www.nationalshareoffice.com

Support for parents and siblings who have experienced pregnancy and infant loss

National SIDS/Infant Death Resource Center

8280 Greensboro Drive Suite 300

McLean, Virginia 22102

(866) 866-7437

Resources for information about sudden infant death syndrome and support for those affected by SIDS

NOVA (National Organization for Victim Assistance)

1757 Park Road NW

Washington, DC 20010

(202) 232-6682

www.try-nove.org

Crisis intervention for victims, support and assistance for survivors of a violent crime

Parents of Murdered Children (POMC)

100 East Eighth Street Suite B-41

Cincinnati, OH 45202

(888) 818-POMC

continued POMC

www.pomc.com

Support for survivors of homicide

Tragedy Assistance Program for Survivors (TAPS)

2001 S Street NW, Suite 300

Washington, DC 20009

(800) 959-8277

www.taps.org

Support and assistance for members of the armed services who experience death and bereavement

NOTES

NOTES